EASY Dollar Bill ORIGAMI

JOHN MONTROLL

DOVER PUBLICATIONS, INC.
MINEOLA, NEW YORK

To Jonathan, Rachel, and Naomi

Copyright

Copyright © 2010 John Montroll
All rights reserved.

Bibliographical Note

Easy Dollar Bill Origami is a new work, first published by Dover Publications, Inc., in 2010.

International Standard Book Number

ISBN-13: 978-0-486-47009-2
ISBN-10: 0-486-47009-1

Manufactured in the United States by Courier Corporation
47009102
www.doverpublications.com

INTRODUCTION

Dollar bill origami has become a very popular form of the art of paperfolding. Here is a collection of dollar bill folds that are easy and fun to fold.

Here is a variety of objects, animals, insects, birds and more, including the fox, rhinoceros, jumping frog, bowtie, and even George Washington himself. While most of the models are my own designs, several have been adapted from traditional origami designs. I would like to thank my friend, Brian Webb, for sharing the bowtie, which he learned to fold from his father.

The diagrams conform to the internationally approved Randlett-Yoshizawa style. The diagrams use different shades of green to represent the two sides of the dollar; you may choose which side you wish to show.

Origami supplies can be found in arts and craft shops, or visit Dover Publications online at www.doverpublications.com, or OrigamiUSA at www.origami-usa.org.

I wish to thank Charley Montroll and Robert Lang for their help. It is my hope that you will receive many hours of enjoyment folding these models.

John Montroll
www.johnmontroll.com

CONTENTS

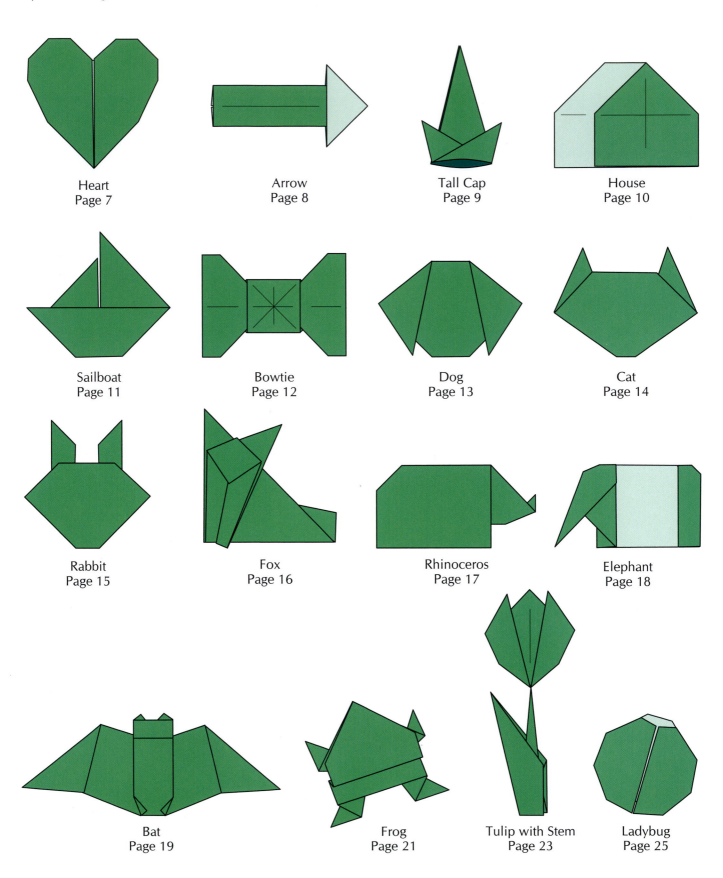

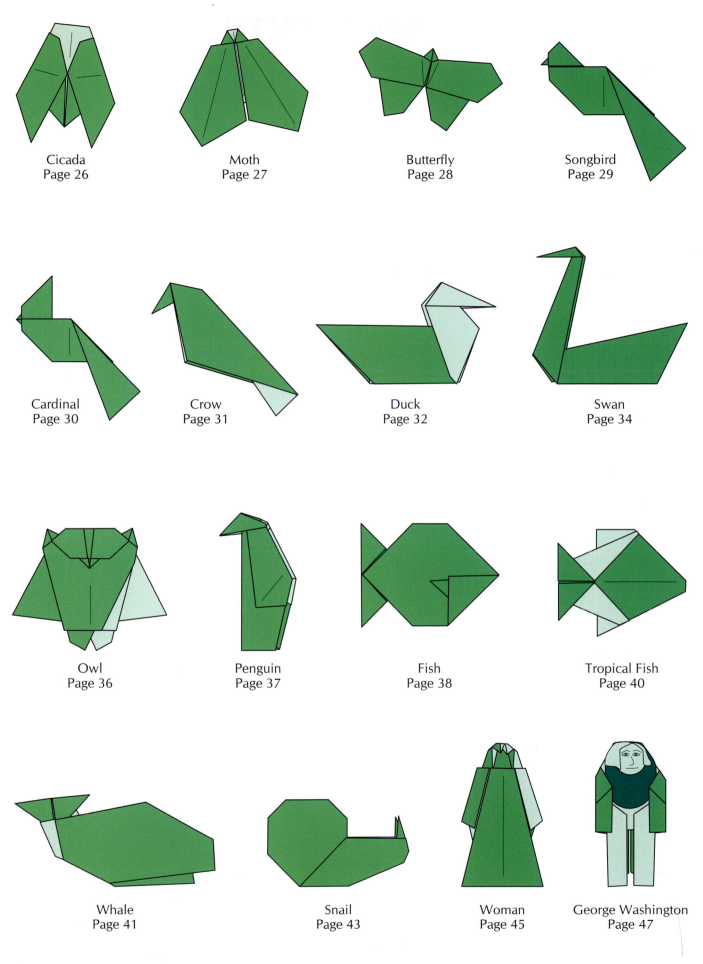

SYMBOLS

Lines

— — — — — — — — — — Valley fold, fold in front.

— · — · — · — · — · — Mountain fold, fold behind.

_____ Crease line.

· X-ray or guide line.

Arrows

Fold in this direction.

Fold behind.

Unfold.

Fold and unfold.

Turn over.

Sink or three dimensional folding.

Place your finger between these layers.

HEART

1

Fold and unfold.

2

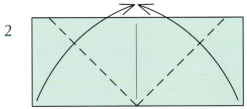

3

4

5

6

7

8

9

Heart

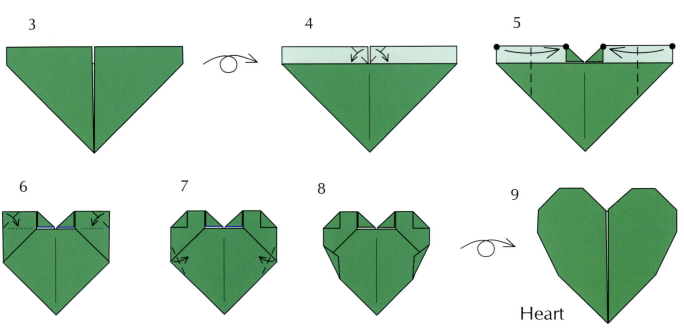

ARROW

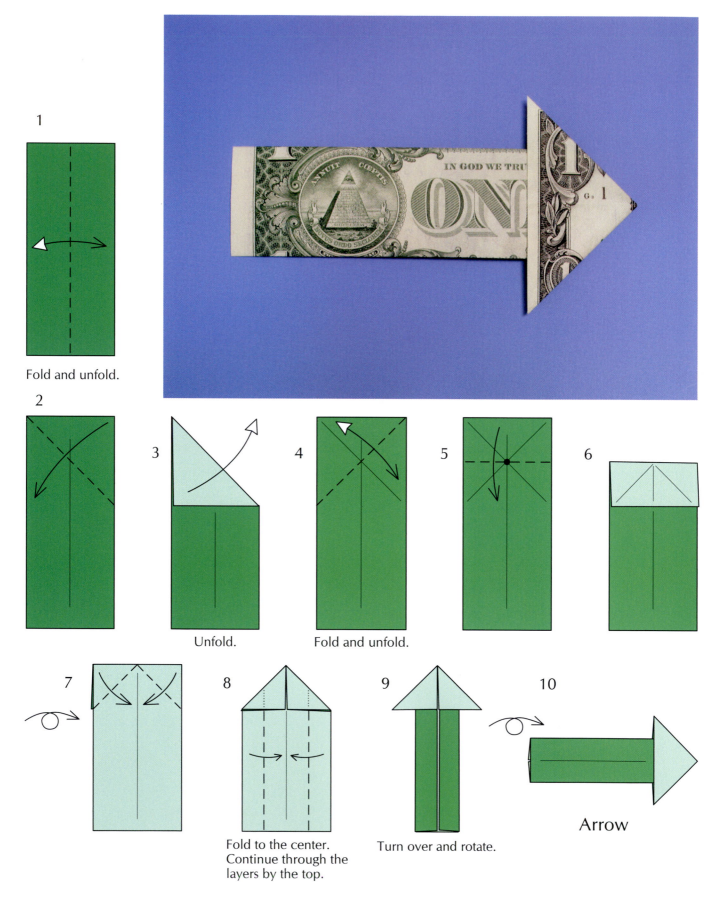

1

Fold and unfold.

2

3

Unfold.

4

Fold and unfold.

5

6

7

8

Fold to the center.
Continue through the
layers by the top.

9

Turn over and rotate.

10

Arrow

TALL CAP

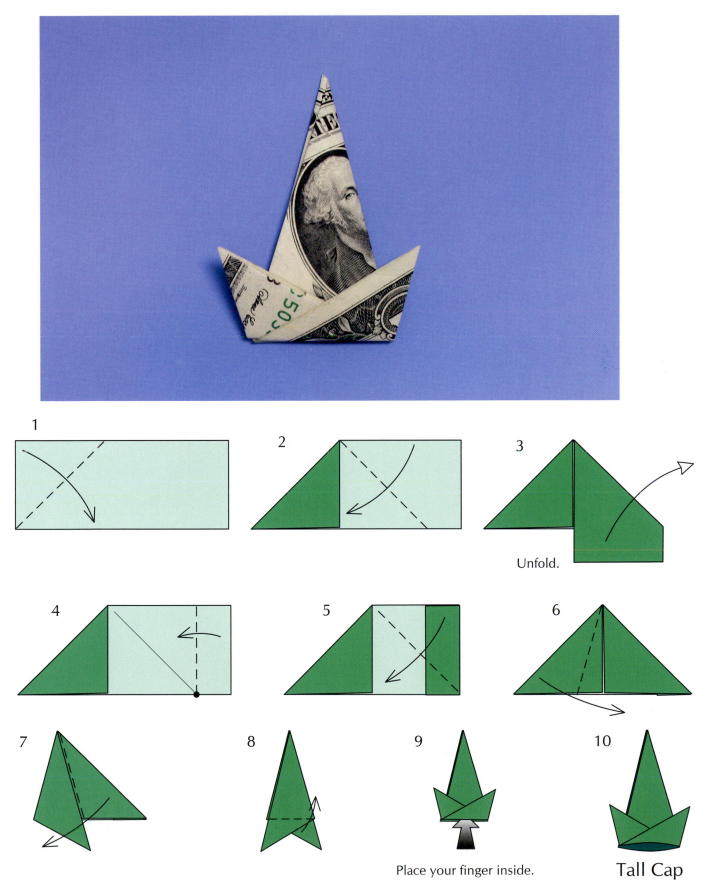

1

2

3

Unfold.

4

5

6

7

8

9

Place your finger inside.

10

Tall Cap

HOUSE

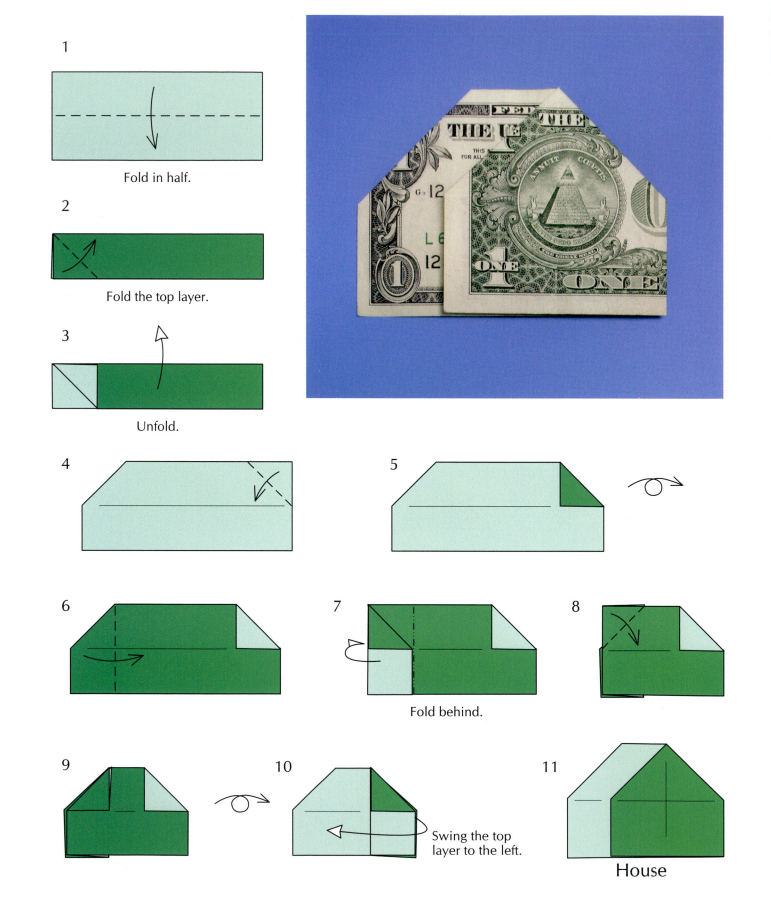

1

Fold in half.

2

Fold the top layer.

3

Unfold.

4

5

6

7

Fold behind.

8

9

10

Swing the top layer to the left.

11

House

SAILBOAT

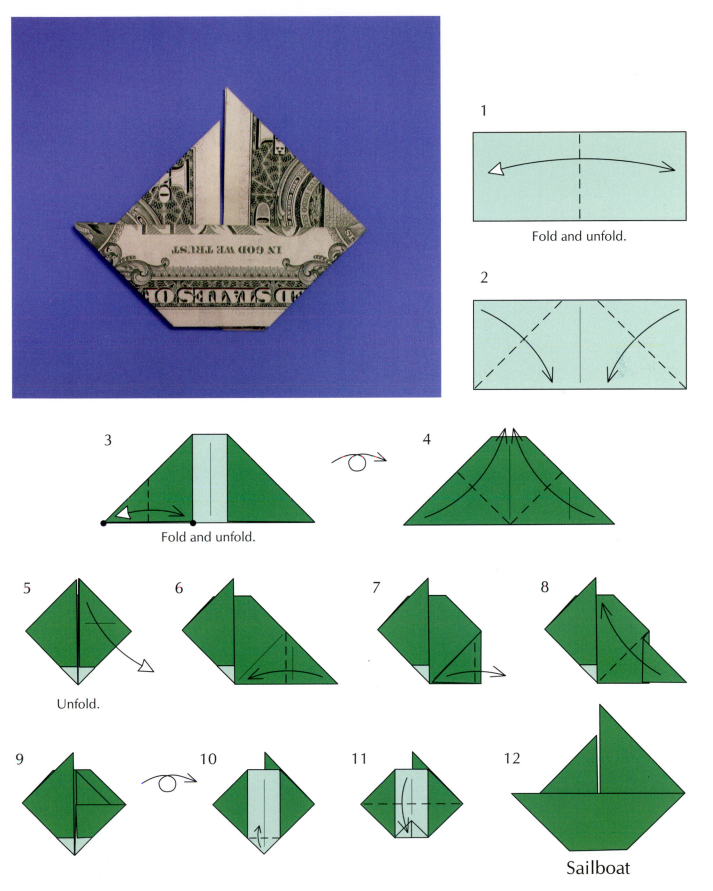

1

Fold and unfold.

2

3

Fold and unfold.

4

5

Unfold.

6

7

8

9

10

11

12

Sailboat

BOWTIE

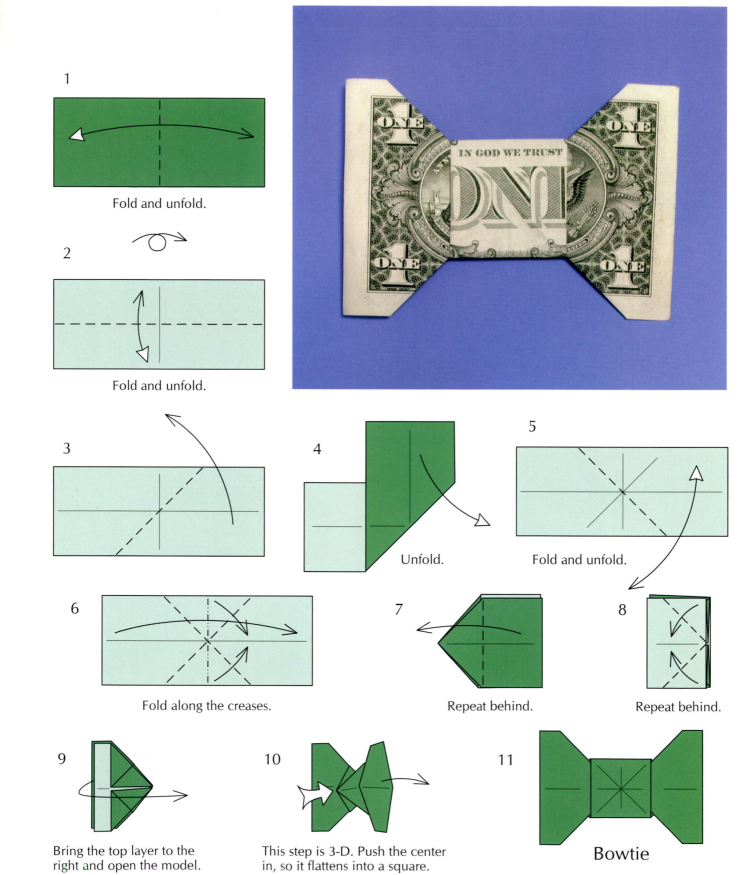

1

Fold and unfold.

2

Fold and unfold.

3

4

Unfold.

5

Fold and unfold.

6

Fold along the creases.

7

Repeat behind.

8

Repeat behind.

9

Bring the top layer to the right and open the model.

10

This step is 3-D. Push the center in, so it flattens into a square.

11

Bowtie

DOG

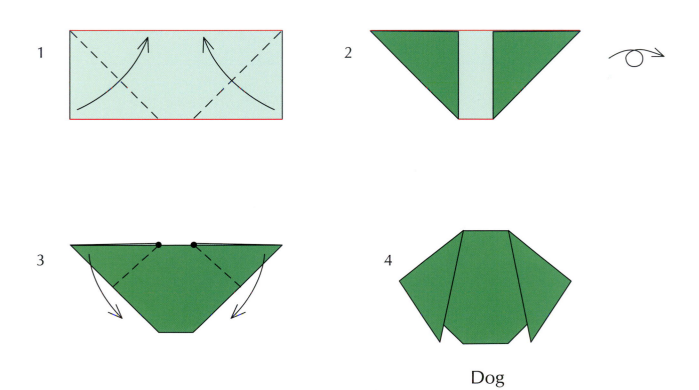

1

2

3

4

Dog

CAT

1 Fold and unfold.

2

3 Fold a thin strip down.

4

5 Fold the tip up.

6

7

Cat

RABBIT

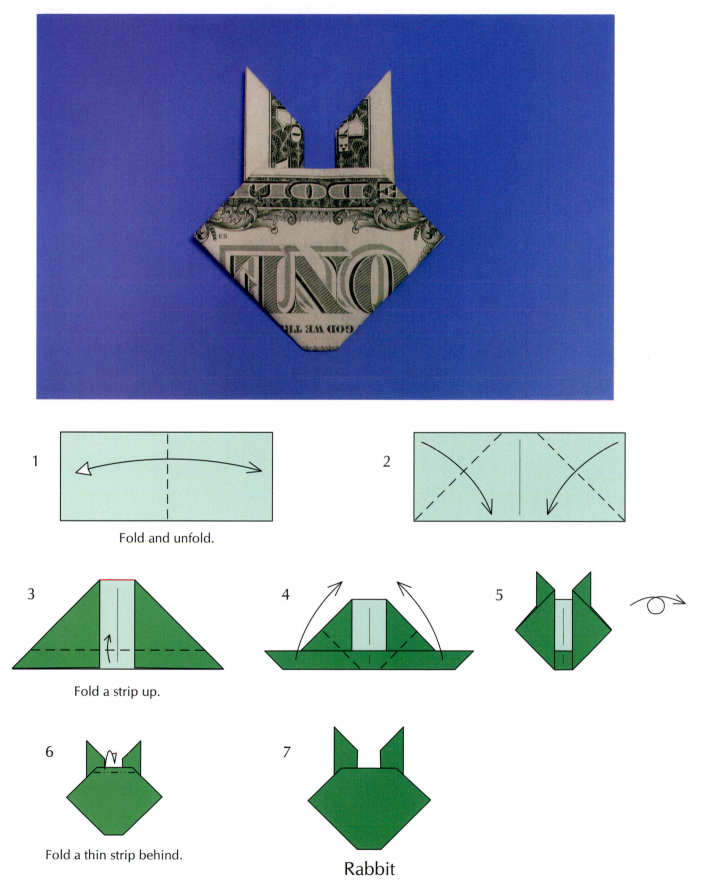

1 Fold and unfold.

2

3 Fold a strip up.

4

5

6 Fold a thin strip behind.

7 Rabbit

FOX

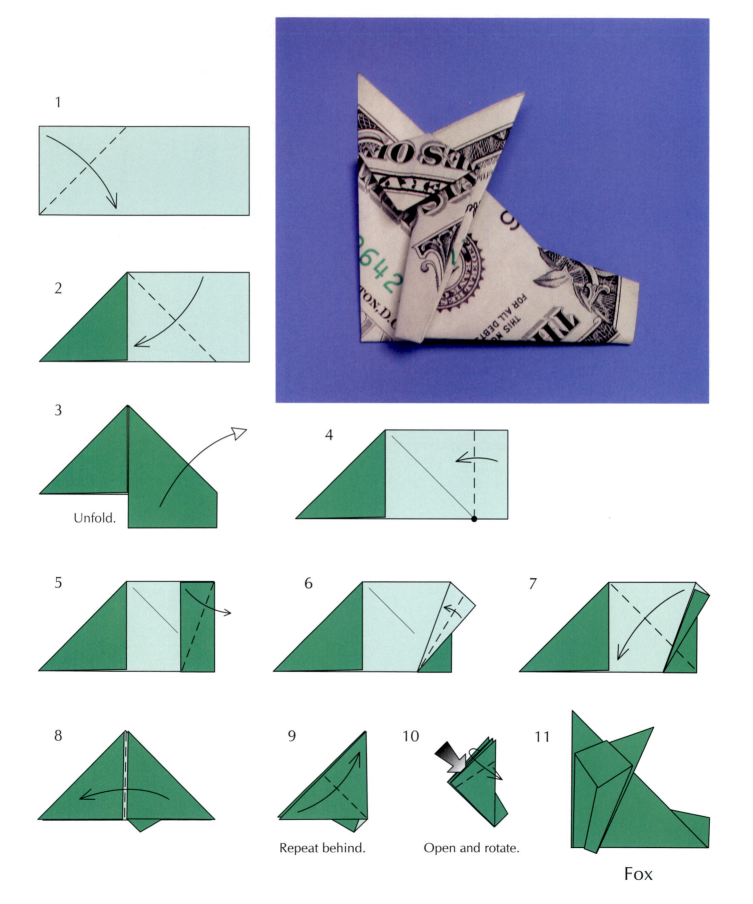

1

2

3

Unfold.

4

5

6

7

8

9

Repeat behind.

10

Open and rotate.

11

Fox

RHINOCEROS

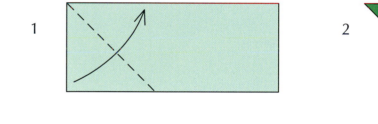

1

2

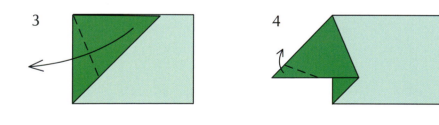

3

4

5

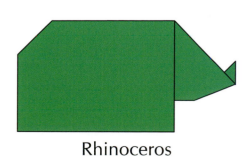

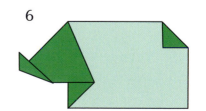

6

7

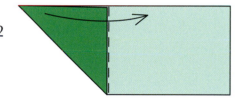

Rhinoceros

ELEPHANT

1

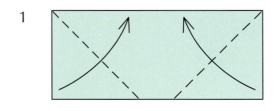

2

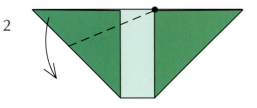

3

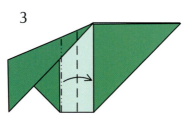

Fold back and forth.

4

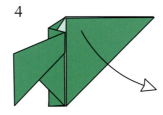

Unfold.

5

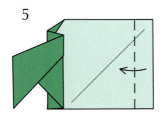

6

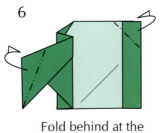

Fold behind at the
trunk and back.

7

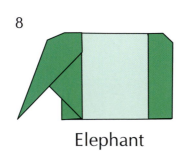

Fold behind.

8

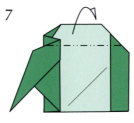

Elephant

BAT

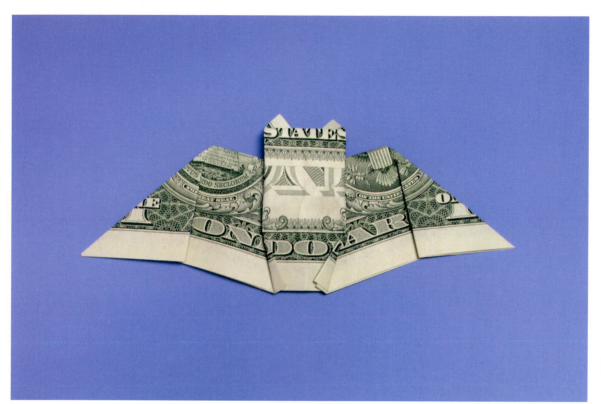

1   Fold and unfold.

2

3

4   Fold to the top and unfold.

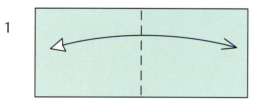
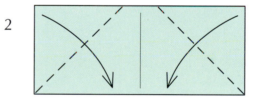

5   Fold up so the horizontal crease matches the upper edge.

6

7

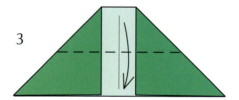
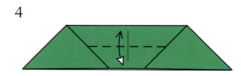

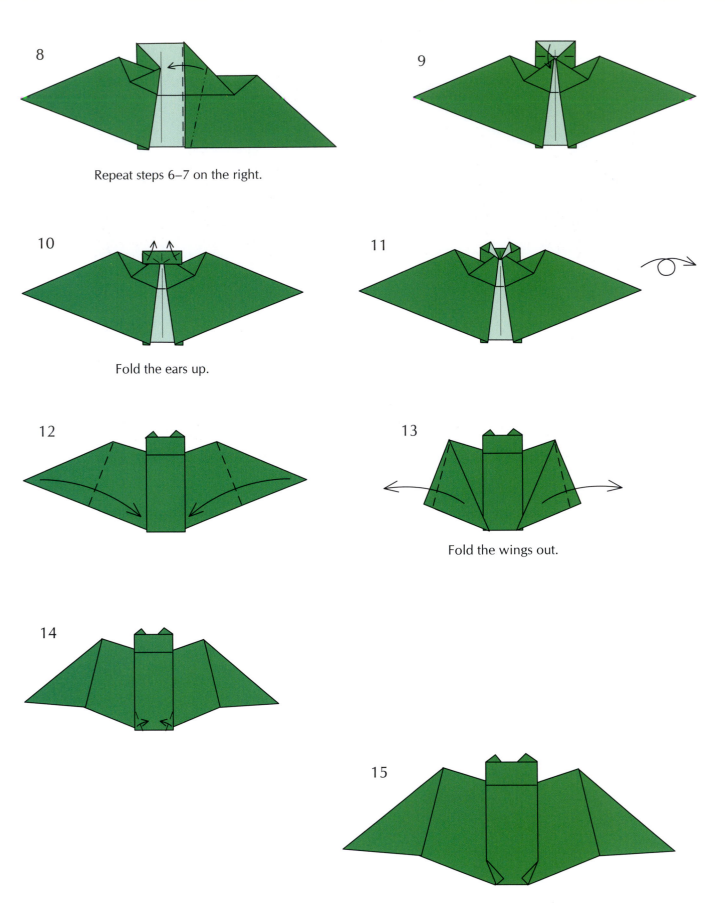

8

Repeat steps 6–7 on the right.

9

10

Fold the ears up.

11

12

13

Fold the wings out.

14

15

Bat

FROG

1 Fold and unfold.

2

3

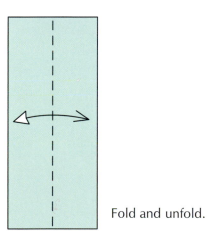

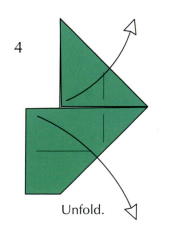

4 Unfold.

5

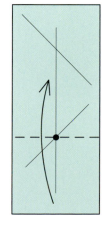

6 Fold and unfold.

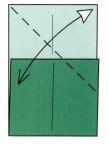

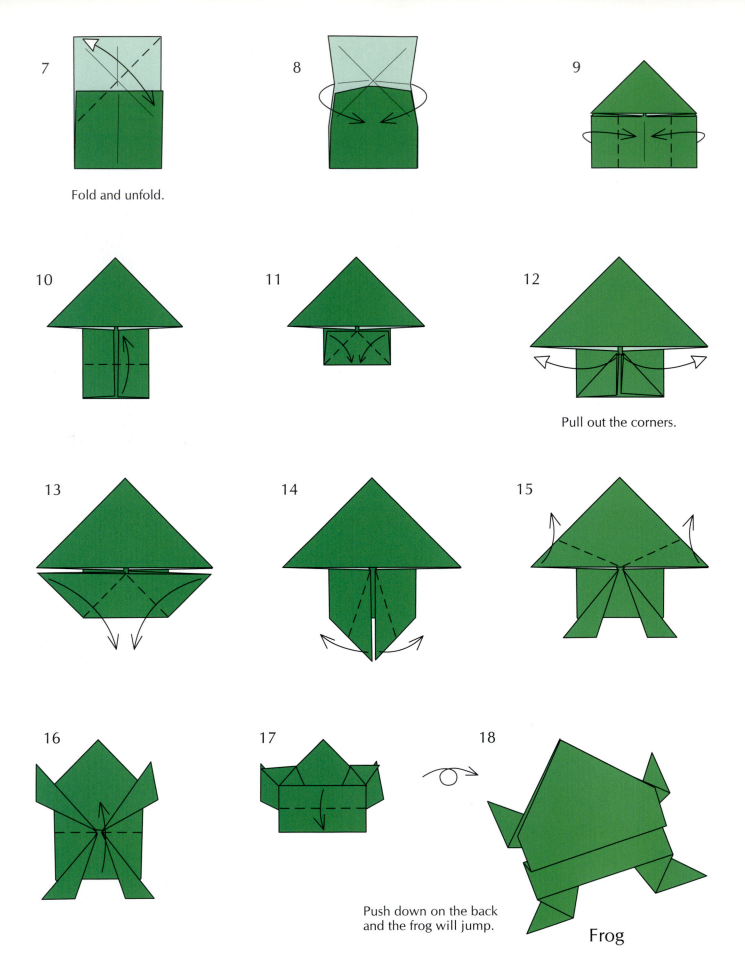

7

Fold and unfold.

8

9

10

11

12

Pull out the corners.

13

14

15

16

17

18

Push down on the back
and the frog will jump.

Frog

TULIP WITH STEM

Tulip

1

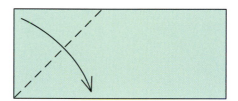

2

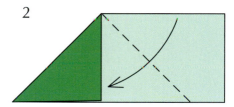

3

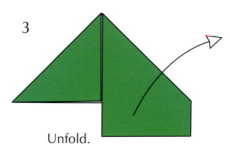

Unfold.

4

5

6

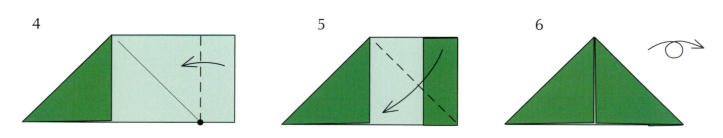

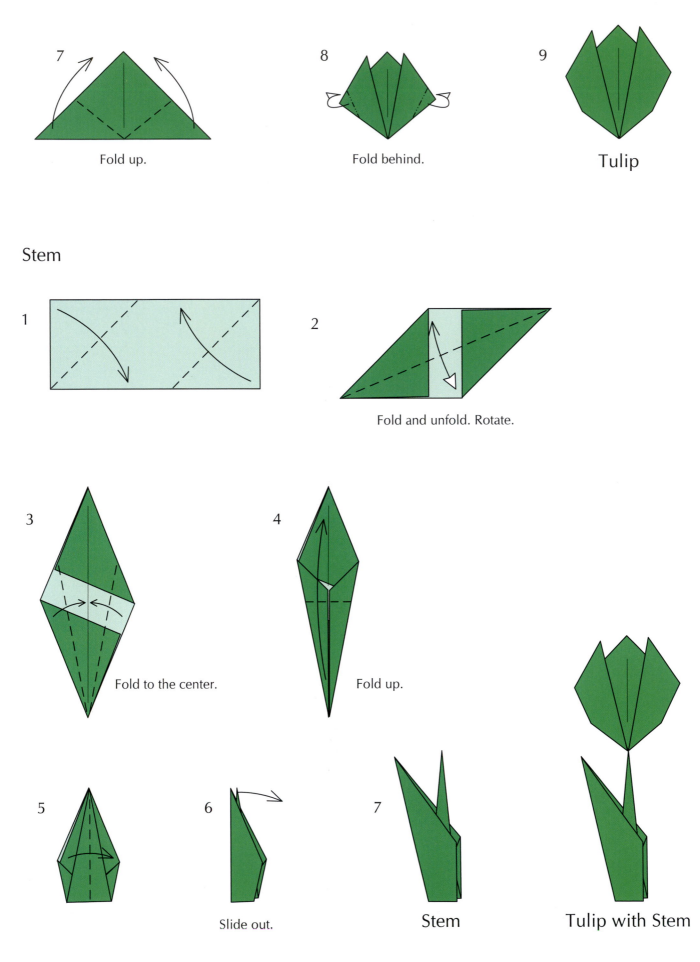

7 Fold up.

8 Fold behind.

9 Tulip

Stem

1

2 Fold and unfold. Rotate.

3 Fold to the center.

4 Fold up.

5

6 Slide out.

7 Stem

Tulip with Stem

LADYBUG

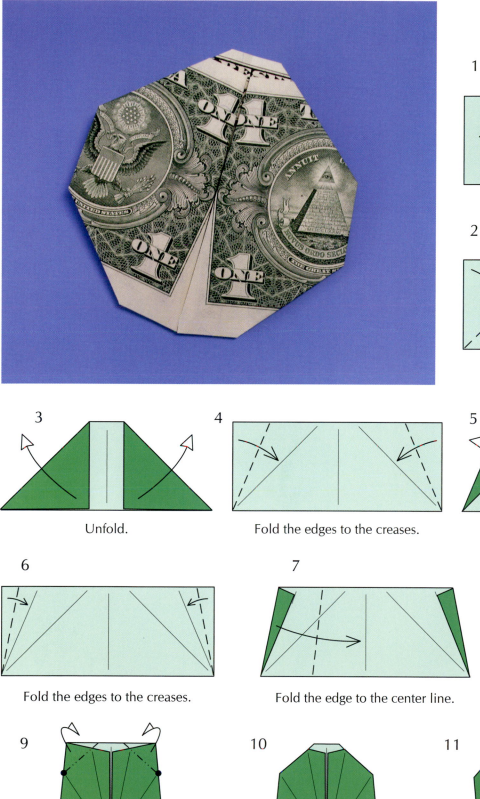

1

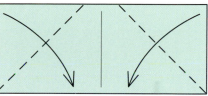

Fold and unfold.

2

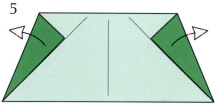

3

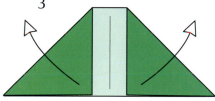

Unfold.

4

Fold the edges to the creases.

5

Unfold.

6

Fold the edges to the creases.

7

Fold the edge to the center line.

8

Fold the edge to the center line.

9

Fold behind.

10

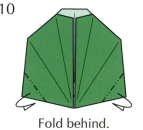

Fold behind.

11

Ladybug

CICADA

1

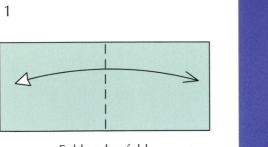

Fold and unfold.

2

Fold and unfold.

3

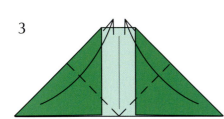

4

Pull out.

5

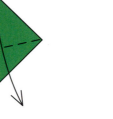

Pull out.

6

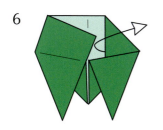

Pull out.

7

Fold inside.

8

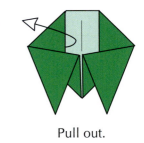

Fold inside.

9

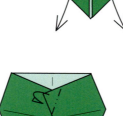

Fold behind.

10

Cicada

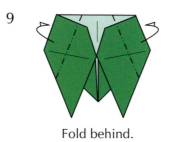

MOTH

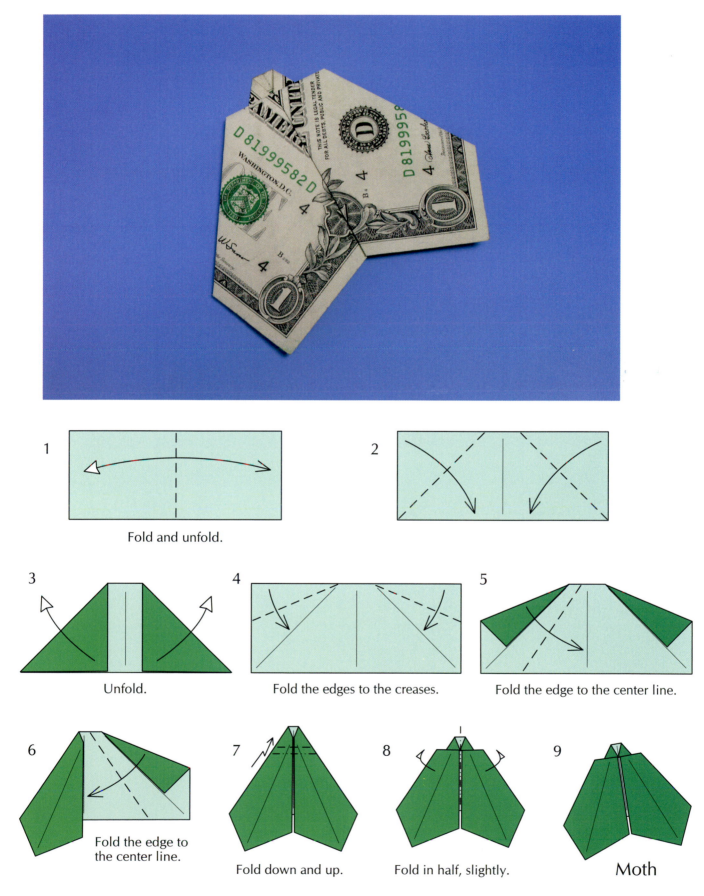

1 Fold and unfold.

2

3 Unfold.

4 Fold the edges to the creases.

5 Fold the edge to the center line.

6 Fold the edge to the center line.

7 Fold down and up.

8 Fold in half, slightly.

9 Moth

BUTTERFLY

1

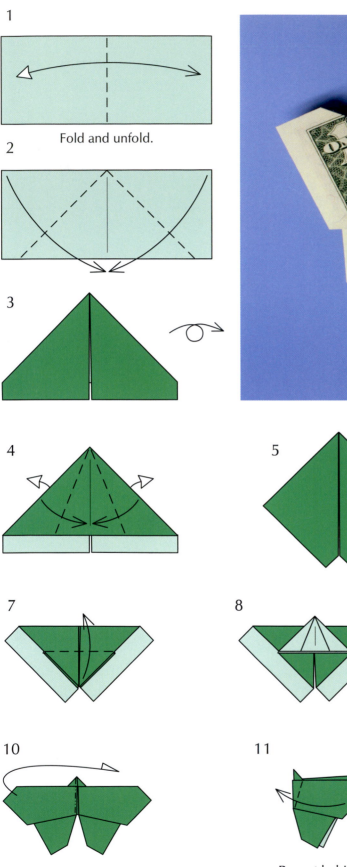

Fold and unfold.

2

3

4

5

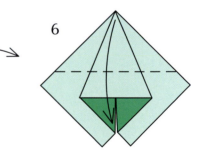

6

7

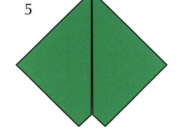

8

9

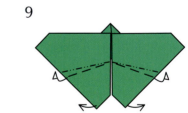

10

11

Repeat behind.

12

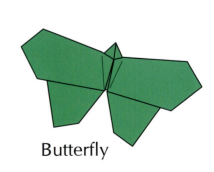

Butterfly

SONGBIRD

1

Fold and unfold.

2

3

4

5

6

7

8

9

10

Fold back and forth.

11

Songbird

CARDINAL

1

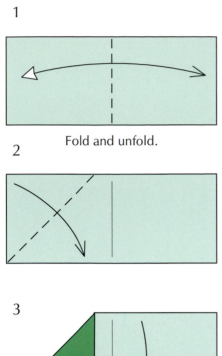

Fold and unfold.

2

3

4

5

6

7

8

9

10

11

Cardinal

CROW

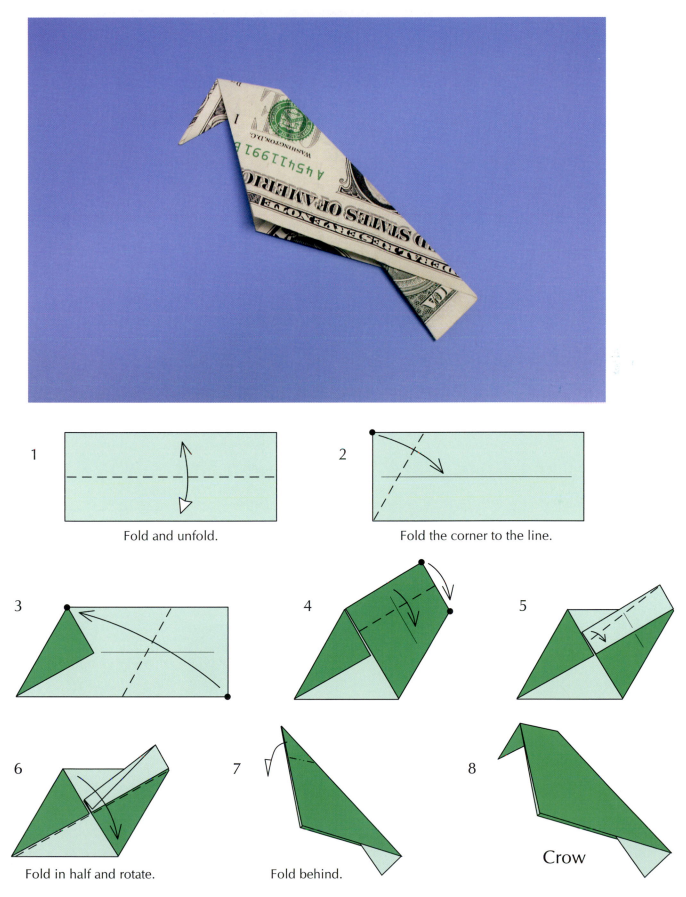

1   Fold and unfold.

2   Fold the corner to the line.

3

4

5

6   Fold in half and rotate.

7   Fold behind.

8   Crow

DUCK

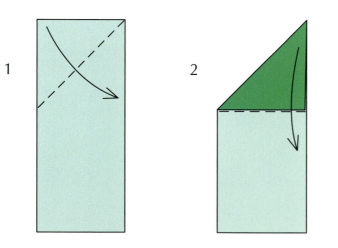

1

2

3

Unfold.

4

Fold and unfold.

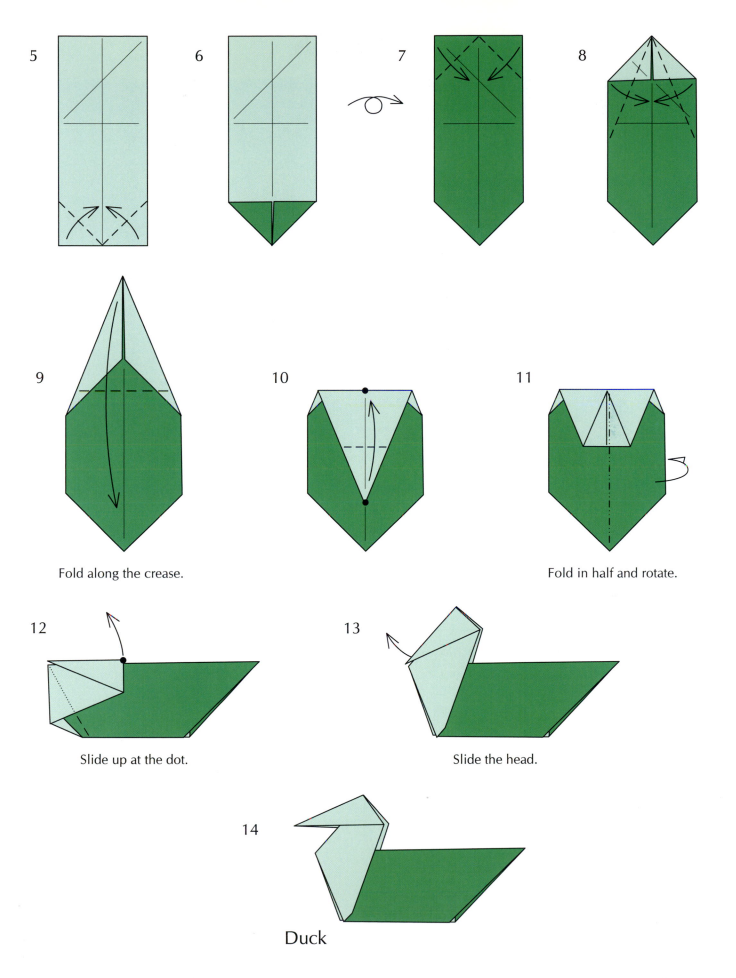

5

6

7

8

9

Fold along the crease.

10

11

Fold in half and rotate.

12

Slide up at the dot.

13

Slide the head.

14

Duck

SWAN

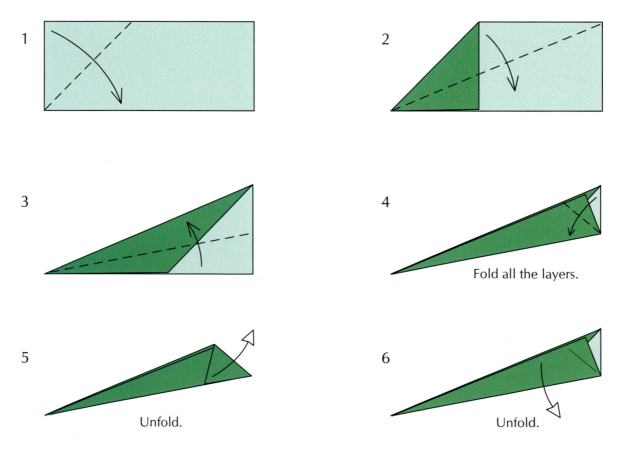

1

2

3

4

Fold all the layers.

5

Unfold.

6

Unfold.

7

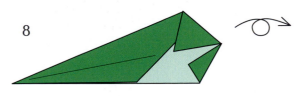

8

Turn over and rotate.

9

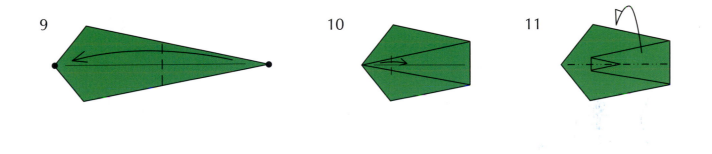

10

11

12

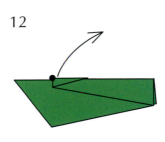

Slide the neck up.

13

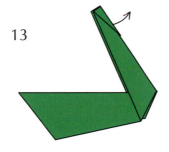

Slide the head up.

14

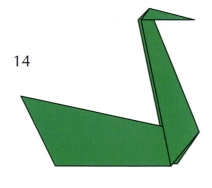

Swan

OWL

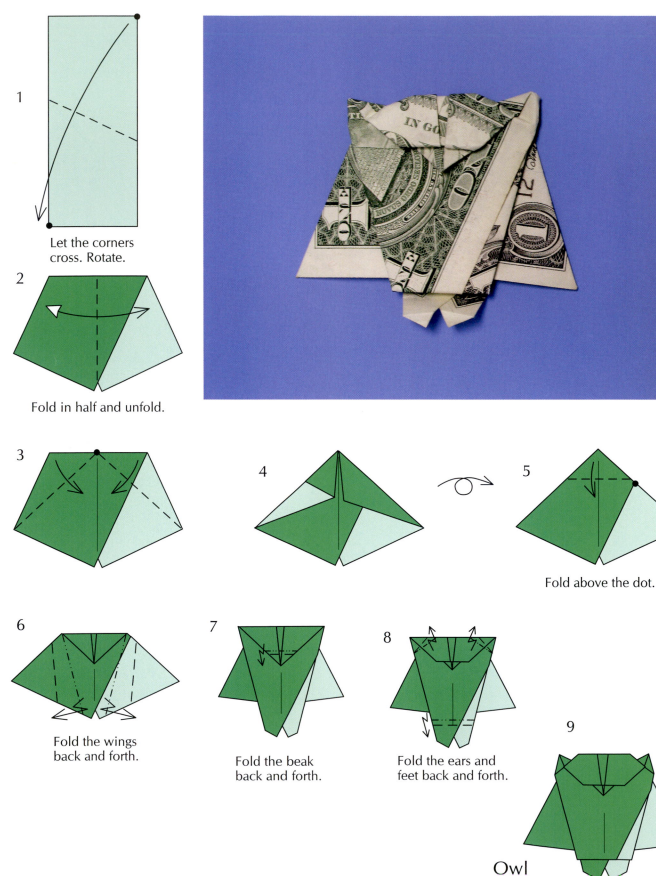

1 Let the corners cross. Rotate.

2 Fold in half and unfold.

3

4

5 Fold above the dot.

6 Fold the wings back and forth.

7 Fold the beak back and forth.

8 Fold the ears and feet back and forth.

9

Owl

PENGUIN

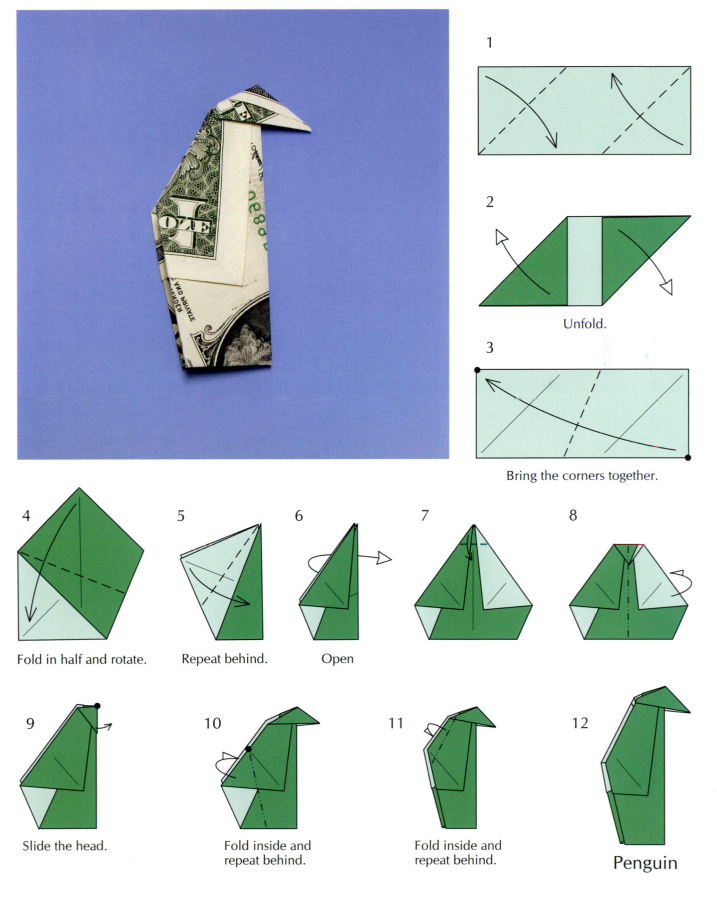

1

2

Unfold.

3

Bring the corners together.

4

Fold in half and rotate.

5

Repeat behind.

6

Open

7

8

9

Slide the head.

10

Fold inside and
repeat behind.

11

Fold inside and
repeat behind.

12

Penguin

FISH

1

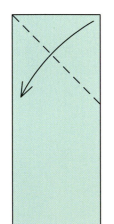

2

Unfold.

3

Fold and unfold.

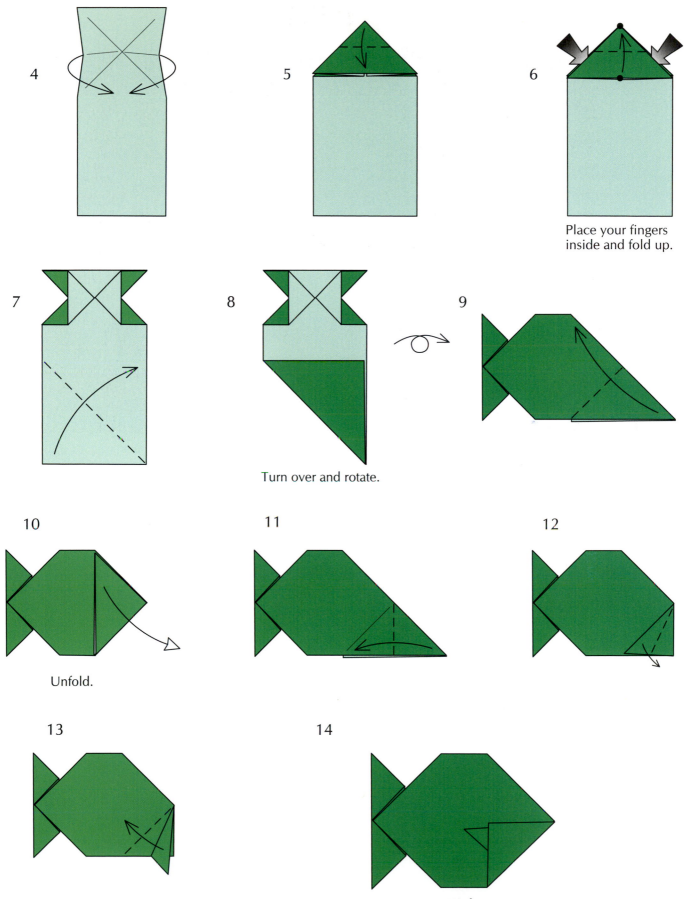

4

5

6

Place your fingers inside and fold up.

7

8

Turn over and rotate.

9

10

Unfold.

11

12

13

14

Fish

TROPICAL FISH

1

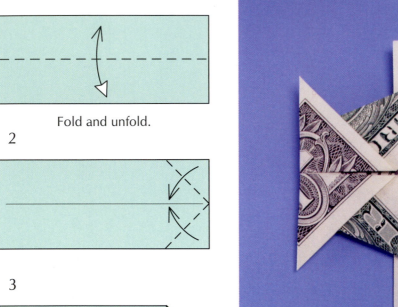

Fold and unfold.

2

3

4

Fold to the center and swing out the corners.

5

6

7

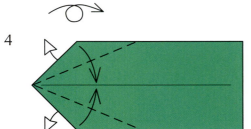

8

9

10

11

Tropical Fish

WHALE

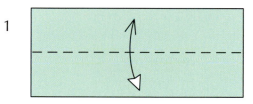

1

Fold and unfold.

2

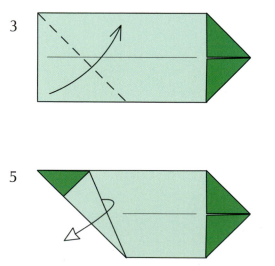

3

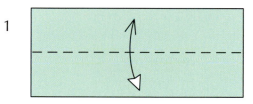

4

5

Unfold.

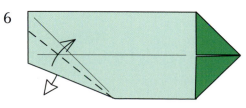

6

Swing out the corner.

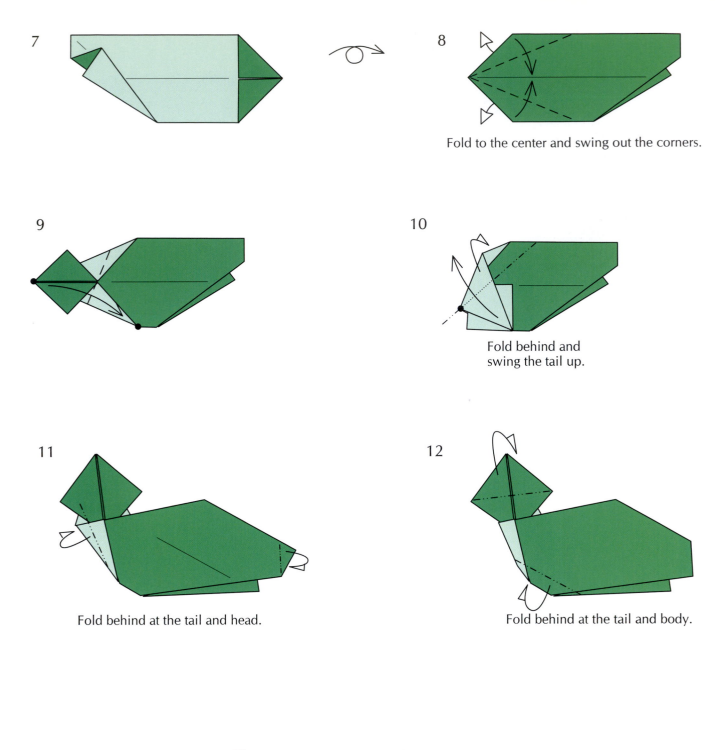

7

8

Fold to the center and swing out the corners.

9

10

Fold behind and
swing the tail up.

11

Fold behind at the tail and head.

12

Fold behind at the tail and body.

13

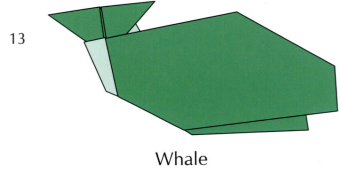

Whale

SNAIL

1

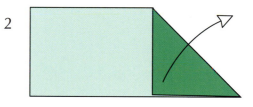

2

Unfold.

3

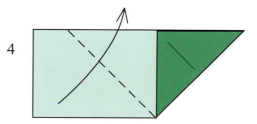

4

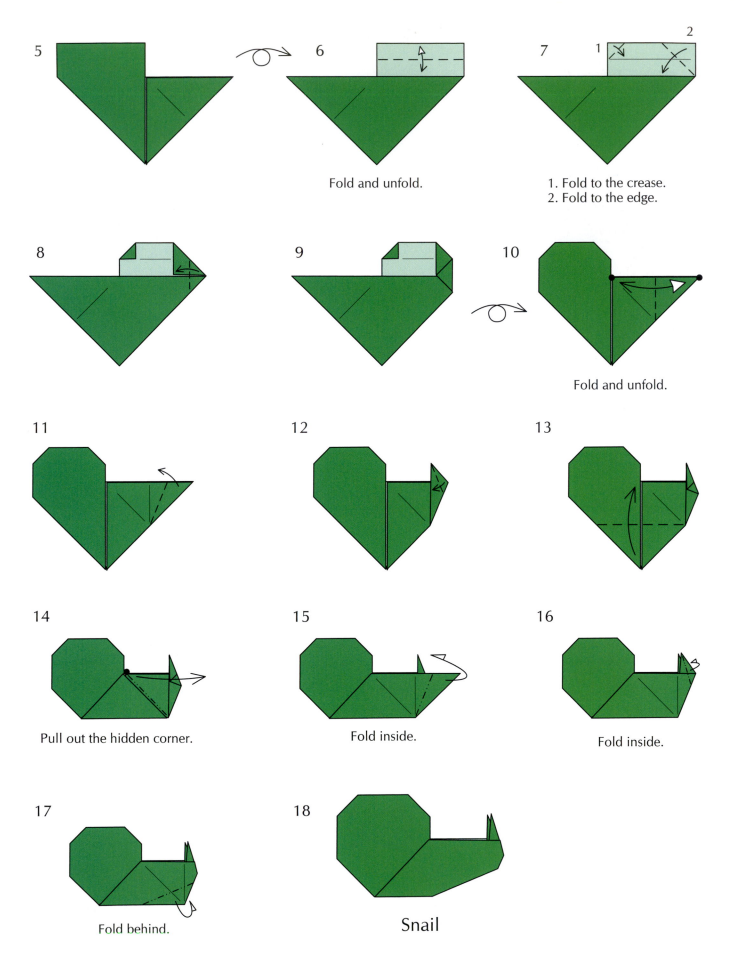

5

6

Fold and unfold.

7

1. Fold to the crease.
2. Fold to the edge.

8

9

10

Fold and unfold.

11

12

13

14

Pull out the hidden corner.

15

Fold inside.

16

Fold inside.

17

Fold behind.

18

Snail

WOMAN

1 Bring the corners together. Rotate.

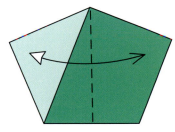

2 Fold and unfold in half.

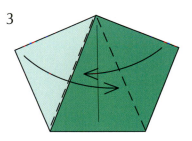

3

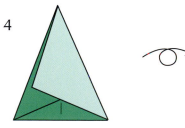

4

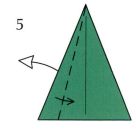

5 Fold close to the center and let the hidden corner swing out.

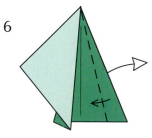

6 Repeat on the right.

7

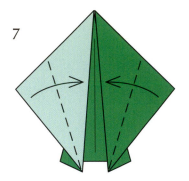

8

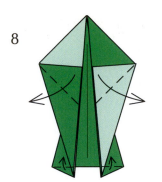

9

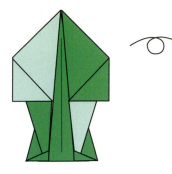

10

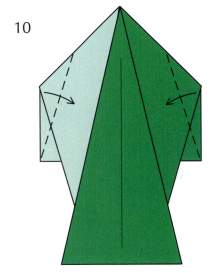

11

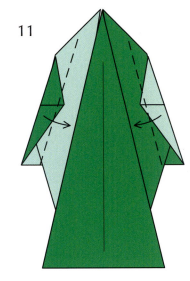

12

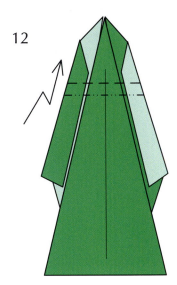

Fold down and up.

13

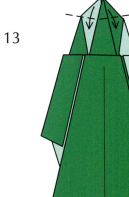

Separate the two corners
while folding down.

14

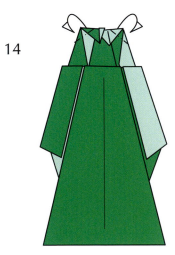

15

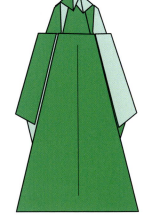

Woman

Begin with George Washington
on the front.

1

Fold and unfold.

2

Fold the corners to the edges.

3

4

Fold towards the center.

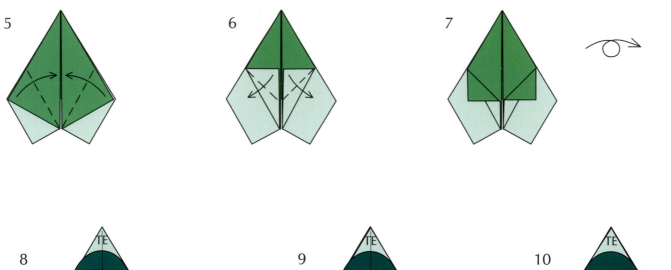

5

6

7

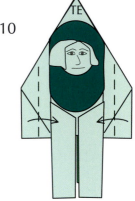

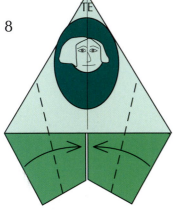

8

Fold the edges to the center.

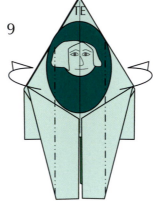

9

Fold inside.

10

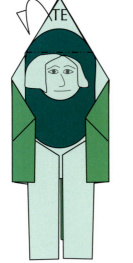

11

Fold the layers behind.

12

13

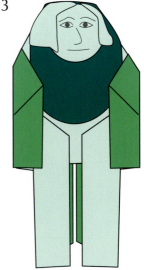

George Washington